Looking For Napoleon!
A Kid's Guide To Ajaccio, Corsica, France

Photography by John D. Weigand
Poetry by Penelope Dyan

Bellissima Publishing, LLC
Jamul, California
www.bellissimapublishing.com

Copyright © 2017 by Penny D. Weigand and John D. Weigand

All rights reserved. No part of this book may be
reproduced or transmitted in any form or by any means,
electronic or mechanical, including photocopying,
recording, or by any other means, or by any information or
storage retrieval system, without permission from the publisher.

.

ISBN 978-1-61477-279-8
First Edition

"It's easier to fool people than to convince them that they have been fooled."

Mark Twain

Napoleon Was Here!
Bellissima Publishing, LLC

Introduction

Ajaccio, the capital city of Corsica declined during the Middle Ages, and recovered after the Genoese built a citadel there in 1492. The Corsican Republic was declared in 1755; and the Genoese continued its holdings, including Ajaccio, until the French took control. The most famous Ajaccio inhabitant was Emperor Napoleon Bonaparte, born here in 1769. His family home, the Maison Bonaparte, is a now grand museum After Napoleon was defeated at the Battle of Leipzig in October 1813, he retreated to Paris; but with little support from his military marshals, he was forced to renounce his throne in April of 1814. The European powers exiled him to Elba Island. However, within eleven months he returned, heading an army that wanted him to retake the French throne. Napoleon's final defeat came June, 1815 at the famous Battle of Waterloo, after which he was exiled to the far off island of St. Helena, a barren, wind-swept rock.

Written by the award winning author, attorney and former teacher, Penelope Dyan, with photography by John D. Weigand this is the perfect 'learn to read' book for you if you want to see where Napoleon was born! When you are finished reading this book, watch the free music video that goes with this book on Bellissimavideo's YouTube channel.

Napoleon Was Here!
Bellissima Publishing, LLC

Looking For Napoleon!
A Kid's Guide To Ajaccio, Corsica, France

Photography by John D. Weigand
Poetry by Penelope Dyan

You arrive at Corsica, at Ajaccio,
the place of Napoleon's birth.
You gaze upon the Mediterranean blue.
Its salty water laps the earth.

Like you and Mom and Dad,
people walk up and down the street.
You notice that one woman
has bright green shoes upon her feet.
You ALWAYS wanted shoes
of bright green,
but whether Mom will EVER
buy you a pair,
is something that remains to be seen.

You turn the corner,
and somehow,
this street appears somewhat
deserted right now.
You wonder what it was like
when Napoleon Bonaparte
was a BOY growing up HERE.
Was Napoleon Bonaparte
a child who knew NO fear?
Or was he a child who ALL night,
kept a lantern lit to have some light?
Did he sleep soundly in the dark,
or did he DREAD
imaginary monsters
lurking UNDER his bed?

You see a seagull resting all alone.
Like Napoleon Bonaparte,
THIS is this seagull's home!
And in this place THIS seagull will stay,
until (like Napoleon Bonaparte)
it flies AWAY!

You see a donkey eating green grass on the ground,
a lovely donkey of shades of brown.

You see a goat living on life's edge,
reaching down to eat
some grass and stuff
growing on a deep, steep ledge!
And it makes you wonder
about up and down,
as you look up and down,
and all around.
Then Mom reminds you,
"Life is sometimes up,
and sometimes it's down.
Just remember to keep
both of YOUR feet on the ground!"

Then you feel a rumbling
in your OWN tummy!
And you, Mom and Dad
find some food to eat that's yummy!
And Mom reminds you
(as usual) that AFTER you eat,
you will all find
something that's sweet!

You see a church, and as you know, this is where you feed your soul!

Then you see a bus painted blue,
that looks like
Napoleon Bonaparte is riding in it,
along with Josephine TOO!
And you laugh and you smile,
because YOU are having fun!
You skip and you jump!
And ahead of Mom and Dad you run!

You stop and see laundry drying
white, green, red, pink and blue.
You wait for Mom and Dad
to catch up with YOU!
And you see a satellite dish!
You wonder if for dinner,
the family (who lives here) will eat fish.
And for a moment you could swear,
that you can smell the smell
of fish frying,
in the Mediterranean air!

And there he is, of course,
Napoleon Bonaparte riding a horse!

Then, next to the Mediterranean blue,
a colorful carousel is waiting for you!
And from the joy of it all
you cannot hide,
as you hop aboard and ride and ride.
And that night,
when you are tucked into your bed,
thoughts of Napoleon Bonaparte
fill up your head.
Mom kisses your forehead.
You scratch your nose. . .
You ask,
"Was Napoleon Bonaparte the emperor
who wore no clothes?"

"Don't listen to the person who has the answers; listen to the person who has the questions."

Albert Einstein

www.ingramcontent.com/pod-product-compliance
Ingram Content Group UK Ltd.
Pitfield, Milton Keynes, MK11 3LW, UK
UKHW060133240426
12048UKWH00002B/26